essential Musicianship for strings

FUNDAMENTAL ensemble concepts

Michael Allen
Robert Gillespie
Pamela Tellejohn Hayes

Table of Contents

ISBN 1-4234-3103-0

HAL•LEONARD® CORPORATION
7777 W. BLUEMOUND RD. P.O. BOX 13819 MILWAUKEE, WI 53213

D Major Rounds

Five Step Round

English Round

Day Is Done

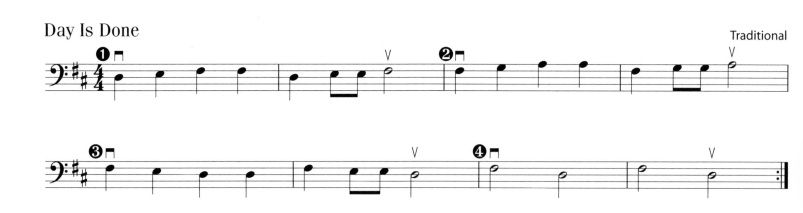

Traditional

Skipping Around

Michael Allen

Port Royal Round

French-Canadian

Arctic Circle

Finland

D Major Arrangements

London Bridge

English Folk Song

Michael Row The Boat Ashore

American Folk Song

Johann Sebastian Bach

Musette

Ode To Joy

Ludwig van Beethoven

Up On The Housetop

Benjamin R. Hanby

Toe Tapping

Michael Allen

Round Dance

German Barndance

G Major Rounds

The Alphabet Song

Old Traditional Song

Hunting Song

Traditional

The Clock

English

Oh, How Lovely Is The Evening

German

G Major Lower Octave (Violin) Arrangements

This Old Man   American Folk Song

Buffalo Gals   American Cowboy Song

Lullaby

Johannes Brahms

Jingli Nona

Far Eastern Folk Song

Friday Night Polka

Michael Allen

C Major Rounds

Classical Round

Franz Joseph Haydn

Silent Woods

American

Stepping Around

English Round
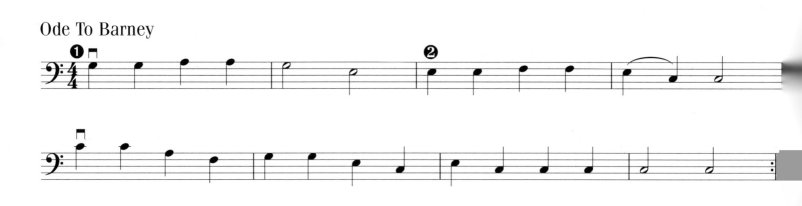

Ode To Barney

Where Is John?

Bedrich Smetana
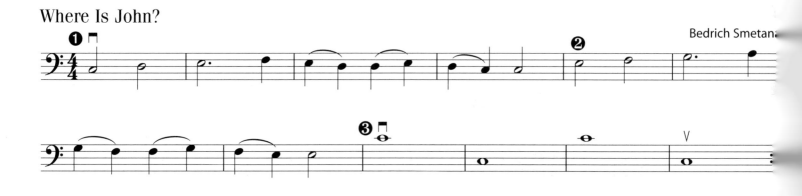

C Major Arrangements

Long, Long Ago

T. H. Bayly

Monday's Melody

Traditional Folk Song

Chanukah

Israeli Folk Song

Blue Bells Of Scotland

Scottish Folk Song

The Orchestra Song – 5 Parts

Old Quodlibet

G Major Rounds

Flying Around

English

Sailing on the Avon

English

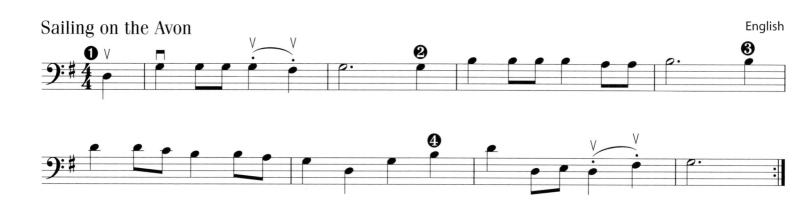

Haste

Samuel Arnold

White Coral Bells

Great Britain

G Major Upper Octave (Violin) Arrangements

Minuet — Johann Sebastian Bach

Cielito Lindo — Mexican Folk Song

The Jolly Boatman

English Folk Song

Botany Bay

Australian Folk Song